Sports Illustrated KIDS

STARS OF SPORTS

BREANNA STEWART

PRO BASKETBALL MVP

by Matt Chandler

CAPSTONE PRESS
a capstone imprint

Stars of Sports is published by
Capstone Press, an imprint of Capstone
1710 Roe Crest Drive, North Mankato, Minnesota 56003
www.capstonepub.com

SPORTS ILLUSTRATED KIDS is a trademark of ABG-SI LLC. Used with permission.

Library of Congress Cataloging-in-Publication Data
Names: Chandler, Matt, author.
Title: Breanna Stewart : pro basketball MVP / Matt Chandler.
Other titles: Pro basketball most valuable player
Description: North Mankato, Minnesota : Captivate is published by Capstone Press, [2021] | Series: SIK Stars of Sports | Includes bibliographical references and index. | Audience: Ages 8-11 years | Audience: Grades 4-6 |
Summary: "Breanna Stewart is a basketball superstar! She dominated in high school. Stewart then went on to play college ball for the UConn Huskies. From there she got the opportunity to play for Team USA in the Olympics-where she scored the winning shot! Readers will learn how Breanna overcame a difficult childhood to go onto achieve her dreams"— Provided by publisher.
Identifiers: LCCN 2021002835 (print) | LCCN 2021002836 (ebook) | ISBN 9781663907158 (Hardcover) | ISBN 9781663907127 (PDF) | ISBN 9781663907141 (Kindle Edition)
Subjects: LCSH: Stewart, Breanna, 1994—Juvenile literature. | Women basketball players—United States—Biography—Juvenile literature. | Basketball players—United States—Biography—Juvenile literature. | Basketball—United States—History—Juvenile literature. | Women's National Basketball Association—History—Juvenile literature.
Classification: LCC GV884.S74 C53 2021 (print) | LCC GV884.S74 (ebook) | DDC 796.323092 [B]—dc23
LC record available at https://lccn.loc.gov/2021002835
LC ebook record available at https://lccn.loc.gov/2021002836

Editorial Credits
Editor: Mandy Robbins; Designer: Dina Her; Media Researcher: Morgan Walters; Production Specialist: Tori Abraham

Image Credits
Associated Press: Cal Sport Media, 11, Cloe Poisson, 21, Daniel Ochoa de Olza, 13, Elaine Thompson, 24, 27, Hans Pennink, 6, Nick Wass, 26, Phelan M. Ebenhack, 28, Tim Roske, 14, 15; Newscom: Bill Shettle/Cal Sport Media, 9, Jeff Wheeler/TNS, 23, Jeffrey Brown/Icon Sportswire DBF, cover, John Woike/MCT, 19, MARK MIRKO, 18, MARK REIS/TNS, 5; Shutterstock: EFKS, 1; Sports Illustrated: David E. Klutho, 16, 17

All internet sites appearing in back matter were available and accurate when this book was sent to press.

TABLE OF CONTENTS

Words in **BOLD** are in the glossary.

OLYMPIC CHAMPION

The United States Women's Basketball team came to the 2016 Olympics as the gold-medal favorites. Breanna Stewart was the youngest member of the American team at 21 years old. Stewart was a **substitute** and the only player who had never played professional basketball.

Team USA faced Spain in the gold-medal game. With a big lead in the fourth quarter, Stewart and the other subs finished off the game. Stewart scored 11 points. Her biggest basket came with 34 seconds left. She drained a three-point shot to put the United States ahead 101–70. They were the final points scored by the Americans in the 2016 Olympics. Stewart had proven she deserved a spot on the team and was a gold-medal winner!

FACT

Stewart has won seven gold medals as a member of the USA Basketball Women's National Team.

>>> Stewart (far left) helps Seimone Augustus (center),
defend against Spain's Anna Cruz in the 2016 Olympics.

>>> Stewart plays during the 2011 New York State Public High School Girls Basketball Championships.

CHAPTER ONE

A YOUNG BALLER

Stewart was born in Syracuse, New York, on August 27, 1994. Back then, her name was Breanna Baldwin. She was raised by her mother, Heather Baldwin.

Growing up, Stewart started out playing softball. But she began to grow taller than all of the other girls. Basketball seemed like a better fit. Her mom signed her up for her first travel team when she was 8 years old. Though she is a superstar today, her former coach, Bob Zywicki, said basketball didn't come easy for Stewart.

"If Bree hadn't been 5 [foot] 7 [inches], Bree probably wouldn't have been on that first travel team," he said in an interview with ESPN. "She wasn't [good]. She had the heart and the desire, but the coordination wasn't there."

When Stewart was 5 years old, her life changed. Her mom began dating Brian Stewart. Brian began to share his love of basketball with Breanna. Soon he married her mom and adopted Breanna. He would take her to the gym to watch him play in a local basketball league.

Stewart credits her strong ballhandling skills to her dad's coaching. He had her dribble around her neighborhood. Each time she would work on a different skill—once left-handed, then once right-handed. Then she would dribble between her legs, and then work on her spin move. By the time she was 12, Stewart was 6 feet (183 centimeters) tall. Her height and improved skills gave her the makings of a future superstar!

>>> Stewart goes up for a jump shot while playing for her high school team.

The hours of dribbling and practicing her shots paid off. Stewart was named a starter on the Cicero North Syracuse High School team as an eighth grader! She was the youngest player on the team. She worked hard to get better.

Stewart's high school coach, Eric Smith, said Stewart was always very determined. "And the great part about coaching her, is that her being great never was something that she thought about," Smith said in a 2016 interview. "It was, 'I need to get better.'"

Stewart did get better. Her height made it easy to get rebounds and block shots. But she wanted to be more than just the tallest player on the team. She kept working with her dad on her shooting skills, and it paid off. As an eighth grader, Stewart scored 9.1 points per game.

>>> Stewart receives the Best Player on the Court award in January 2012.

Stewart continued to grow as a basketball player. Her coach and teammates took notice. "Every year she was the most improved player," Coach Smith said.

Stewart led her high school squad to a state championship in 2011. She was also a star on the Under-16 (U16) United States National Team. She led the USA Under-19 (U19) World Championship Team to a gold medal in Chile too. She even played for the 2011 USA Pan American Games Team.

FACT

Stewart played so well in 2011, she earned her first of three USA Basketball Player of the Year awards.

USA Basketball

Most 14-year-olds are worried about getting good grades and hanging out with their friends. At 14, Stewart was named to the 2009 USA Women's National Team in the U16 division. That year she averaged 9.6 points per game at the International Basketball Federation (FIBA) U16 Americas Championship. As a member of Team USA, Stewart spent her teenage years traveling the world. She played in France, Spain, and other countries.

⟩⟩⟩ Stewart blocks a shot against Argentina's Rocio Diaz.

Stewart saved her best play for her senior season. As the star of her high school team, she **dominated** her opponents. She averaged 26 points and nearly 14 **rebounds** per game.

〉〉〉 Stewart tries to block a shot by her opponent in the 2012 New York State Girls Basketball Championship.

FACT

Stewart was named the Gatorade National Girls Basketball Player of the Year her senior year of high school.

In the 2012 semifinals of the New York State Federation Tournament, Stewart scored 42 points and pulled down 23 rebounds. She led her team to an 80-55 win over Nazareth Regional High School. It was her shot in the first quarter that stole the show. With time running out, Stewart grabbed a rebound and threw up a shot from her own end of the court. From more than 50 feet (15 meters) away, she drained the shot at the buzzer! Stewart finished her senior season by leading her team to back-to-back state titles.

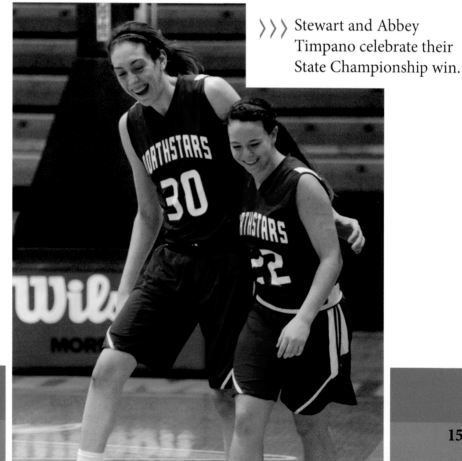

>>> Stewart and Abbey Timpano celebrate their State Championship win.

CHAPTER THREE

COLLEGE BALL

Stewart was one of the highest **recruited** female basketball players in the country. She grew up rooting for her hometown team, the Syracuse Orange. They wanted her to play there. She was also recruited to play for the University of Connecticut (UConn) Huskies. Stewart felt an instant connection with UConn Coach Geno Auriemma. In the end, Stewart chose UConn.

〉〉〉 Stewart in action for the UConn Huskies

〉〉〉 Stewart (left) cheers on her teammates from the sidelines.

Though she liked her coach, Stewart struggled as a freshman. The pace of college games seemed too much for her. She began missing shots and getting beat on defense.

"I couldn't figure things out, and it was frustrating because I didn't know what to do," Stewart said.

"Emotionally, she was not prepared for her first taste of failure," Coach Auriemma said.

Some players might have given up. Not Stewart. She dug in and worked even harder.

By the end of the season, Stewart went from being a struggling player to getting named Most Outstanding Player (MOP) of the National Collegiate Athletic Association (NCAA) Final Four! Those are the last four teams playing in the NCAA Championship Tournament.

For the next three seasons, Stewart was considered the best player in women's college basketball. She finished her college career as the only player—man or woman—to ever block 400 shots and have 400 **assists**. She led the Huskies to a four-season record of 151-5.

〉〉〉 Stewart comes out of a 2013 UConn game.

>>> Stewart (far right) is named to the 2014 All-American team.

Best of all, Stewart won her final NCAA Championship by beating her hometown Syracuse Orange in 2016. As usual, she led the team in scoring with 24 points. She added 10 rebounds and six assists in the championship game. Stewart's college career ended with a championship. Now she was ready to play professional basketball!

FACT

Stewart was the first woman in history to win four Most Outstanding Player (MOP) awards in a row.

CHAPTER FOUR

LIFE IN THE WNBA

Stewart was the **unanimous** choice to be the Seattle Storm's number one pick in the 2016 Women's National Basketball Association (WNBA) **Draft**. She was about to experience a new kind of basketball. In her past four seasons, the Huskies had only lost five games. The Storm lost 24 games in 2015 alone.

Stewart played her first pro game on May 15 against the Los Angeles Sparks. She led the team in scoring with 23 points.

Stewart's best game of the year came in June against the Atlanta Dream. She scored a career-high 38 points. With the Storm trailing by two in the final minute, Stewart made a layup and was fouled. That gave her one foul shot, which she made. Her three-point play gave the Storm the win.

 Stewart (right) stands with Lisa Borders, former WNBA President, after being chosen by the Seattle Storm as the number one draft pick.

FACT

Stewart ended her first year as a pro by being named WNBA **Rookie** of the Year.

WNBA STAR

By 2018, Stewart was a superstar in the WNBA. She started all 34 games for the Storm. She averaged a career-high 21.8 points per game. With the help of her strong play, the Storm finished the season with a record of 26–8.

Stewart didn't slow down in the playoffs. The Storm were tied 2–2 with the Phoenix Mercury. The winner of Game 5 would advance to the WNBA Finals. Her team needed Stewart to step up. She delivered. Stewart was the only Storm player to play the entire game. She led the team with 28 points. The Storm won 94–84.

Stewart stayed hot in the Finals, averaging about 25 points per game. She led the Storm to an easy sweep of the Washington Mystics. The Seattle Storm were the WNBA Champions!

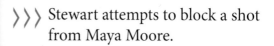

⟩⟩⟩ Stewart attempts to block a shot from Maya Moore.

Unfair Pay

In 2018, Stewart was paid $56,793 to play for the Storm. Men playing in the NBA made at least $838,464. This difference in pay seemed very unfair to WNBA players and their fans. Stewart and many other players earn extra money playing overseas for teams in China and Russia during the WNBA **off-season**. But playing that much puts players in greater danger of getting injured. In 2020, the WNBA increased the average player's salary to $100,658.

〉〉〉 Stewart was applauded from the stands during a 2019 game while she was recovering from an injury.

UPS AND DOWNS

In 2019, Stewart tore her **Achilles tendon** playing overseas in the off-season. The injury made her miss the 2019 WNBA season.

In 2020, she returned to a very different basketball world. On the plus side, the WNBA had increased payments. Stewart signed a two-year contract with the Storm averaging $187,750 per year. On the downside, the **COVID-19 pandemic** hit. It forced WNBA players to play the 2020 season in a bubble. They couldn't physically interact with anyone outside of their league—including their families.

Through it all, Stewart scored nearly 20 points per game for the Storm in 2020. She led the Storm in points, rebounds, blocks, and three-point shooting. She ended her season by leading the Storm to a huge win of 92–59 in the WNBA Finals.

CHAPTER FIVE

A FANTASTIC FUTURE

Stewart already has two WNBA titles. She was named Most Valuable Player (MVP) of the 2020 WNBA Finals. That success has led to opportunities off the court for the WNBA's biggest star.

Since turning pro in 2016, Stewart has built a career as more than a player. She signed an **endorsement** deal with Nike. She has written articles fighting for women's rights and mental health awareness.

⟩⟩⟩ Stewart poses with her awards after the 2018 WNBA Finals.

Stewart has also spoken out for causes she cares about. She has pushed to increase voter registration. She has spoken out against police violence. Stewart says she understands her role as an athlete gives her a chance to fight for everyone. "Equality for all takes each of us making an effort," she said. "Together, let's be better."

LOOKING AHEAD

What does the future hold for Breanna Stewart on the basketball court? She continues to be a powerful player on the court. She stayed healthy in 2020 and led the Storm to the WNBA title.

Stewart continues to play for international teams during the WNBA off-season. The more she plays, the more she risks getting injured again. But it also keeps her at the top of her game. Perhaps she will prove what many of her biggest fans believe—Stewart will retire as the best player in the history of women's basketball!

〉〉〉 Stewart stuffs Emma Cannon as she tries to make a shot.

TIMELINE

1994 Breanna Mackenzie Baldwin (later Stewart) is born on August 27 in Syracuse, New York.

2011 Stewart is named USA Basketball Player of the Year.

2012 Stewart is named the Gatorade National Girls Basketball Player of the Year.

2013 Stewart wins the first of four NCAA Championships with UConn.

2014 Stewart wins a gold medal at the FIBA World Championship.

2016 Stewart wins an Olympic gold medal in Brazil as a member of Team USA.

2016 Stewart is selected as the first overall pick in the WNBA Draft by the Seattle Storm.

2016 Stewart is named Rookie of the Year in the WNBA.

2017 Stewart is named to her first WNBA All-Star Team.

2018 Stewart is named WNBA League MVP.

2018 Stewart leads the Storm to the WNBA title in her third season and is named the Finals MVP.

2019 Stewart is named EuroLeague MVP.

2020 Stewart wins second WNBA title.

GLOSSARY

ACHILLES TENDON (uh-KILL-eez TEN-duhn)—a strong, thick cord of tissue that joins the calf muscle to the heel

ASSIST (uh-SIST)—a pass that leads to a score by a teammate

COVID-19 PANDEMIC (KOH-vid-nine-TEEN pan-DEH-mik)—a very contagious and sometimes deadly virus that spread worldwide in 2020

DOMINATE (DAH-muh-nayt)—to rule; in sports, a team or person dominates if they win much more than anyone else

DRAFT (DRAFT)—an event in which athletes are picked to join sports organizations or teams

ENDORSEMENT (in-DORS-muhnt)—the act of an athlete wearing, promoting, or using a product, often times for money

OFF-SEASON (OFF-see-zuhn)—the time of year when a certain activity is not taking place

REBOUND (REE-bound)—the act of gaining possession of the ball after a missed shot

RECRUIT (ri-KROOT)—to ask someone to join a college team

ROOKIE (RUK-ee)—a first-year player

SUBSTITUTE (SUHB-stuh-toot)—a back-up player

UNANIMOUS (yoo-NAN-uh-muhss)—agreed on by everyone

READ MORE

Chandler, Matt. *Pro Basketball Records: A Guide for Every Fan.* North Mankato, MN: Compass Point Books, 2019.

Jankowski, Matt. *The Greatest Basketball Players of All Time.* New York: Gareth Stevens Publishing, 2020.

Omoth, Tyler. *The WNBA Finals.* North Mankato, MN: Capstone Press, 2020.

INTERNET SITES

Breanna Stewart: Official Website
breannastewart.com

Seattle Storm
storm.wnba.com

WNBA
wnba.com

INDEX